Booking the Library

A Guide for Entertainers, Musicians, Speakers and Authors

JESSICA BRAWNER

Booking the Library

ISBN: 0692350187

ISBN-13: 978-0692350188

Published by Story of the Month Club
Denver, CO

Story of the Month Club Edition 2015
Printed in the USA
www.storyofthemonthclub.com

DEDICATION

For all of the hard working performers, entertainers,
musicians and librarians that I have had the privilege to
work with over the years.
This is for you. I wish you all the best in your art.

CONTENTS

ACKNOWLEDGMENTS

With many thanks to Stephanie Bettman, and Luke Halpin for excellent dinner conversations and brainstorming, to Kerry Grombacher who read and offered suggestions and stuck with the agency from beginning to end, and to everyone else who helped smooth the path along the way.

INTRODUCTION

For many years I ran a booking agency dedicated to helping smaller acts increase their annual pay while filling up some of the 'free time' associated with touring. Yes I know 'free time' is a myth for any self-employed person, however in the case of touring performers that time between gigs while you're on the road, stuck in a hotel room, is essentially 'free time.'

In addition to helping performers, the secondary purpose of my agency was to promote cultural and educational entertainment to underserved communities throughout the United States. One of the best ways to reach those communities was through the public library system. 'Wait, what do you mean?' you ask. 'I thought libraries were just about books…?'

In fact, public libraries provide a myriad of services such as: traditional book lending, public concerts, classes, story-time for toddlers, historical interpreters, songwriting workshops etc. If you haven't checked out your public library lately, you really should. The library is a wonderful resource for the community, and an invaluable tool for the self-employed, and small business owners.

As it happens, in addition to providing these services to

the general public, many libraries hire performers, educators, and entertainers to give one to two hour presentations to their patrons. And in many cases, they are willing to pay for those services.

This book discusses the basics of touring, and booking gigs at libraries. It is intended as a resource for musicians, storytellers, puppeteers, authors and other 'living wage' entertainers. Living wage entertainers are those who make their primary living performing but have not yet been 'discovered' by a big name company that will take over promoting and scheduling their appearances. If you fall into this category of performer, this book is for you, to aid in finding new markets, new fans, and new ways of making your living.

We start out with the specifics of libraries, and then move to the basics of touring. I have included blank pages at the end of most chapters as a place for you to take notes and record your thoughts. As a note, I use the words presentation, show and performance interchangeably throughout. Chapters are organized by topic.

As always, I wish you the best in your art.

LIBRARY BASICS

Why libraries? Are you and libraries right for each other?

There are many good reasons to perform at libraries from the altruistic to the mercenary. On the altruistic side – you are providing music, education, culture, or learning experiences to the general population, at no cost to them. The library pays for it, not the attendees. On the mercenary side – you get paid well to perform in a smoke free environment for friendly people, many of whom will join your mailing list and buy your CD's or other products. Even if the audience doesn't show up, you still get paid. You will know your schedule months in advance, and it is quite possible to make a living performing just at libraries and schools as long as you don't have excessive expenses (like a mortgage).

On the facing page are statistics for you – not too many, I promise. This is a list of the top fifteen libraries in the United States based on the number of programs that they put on or host per year. (Note: this list does not differentiate on types of programs – some are put on by the librarians such as story time, or early childhood literacy programs, some are paid performers.) This information was collected from the Institute of Museum and Library Services 2012 Public Libraries Survey.

Library Name	Total Library Programs	Total Program Attendance	Children's Program Attendance
New York Public Library, The Branch Libraries, NY (Library Of Interest)	58,289	1,214,726	645,247
Brooklyn Public Library, NY	40,911	799,708	509,024
Queens Borough Public Library, NY	35,363	660,149	294,662
Free Library Of Philadelphia, PA	24,385	716,070	454,400
San Diego County Library, CA	22,807	504,755	319,121
Multnomah County Library, OR	22,130	311,177	271,039
Orange County Library District, FL	21,761	289,740	131,303
Columbus Metropolitan Library, OH	21,568	381,739	274,993
Cincinnati And Hamilton County, Pl Of, OH	20,964	479,400	393,099
Cuyahoga County Public Library, OH	18,407	380,134	256,950
County Of Los Angeles Public Library, CA	17,785	495,965	431,929
Harris County Public Library, TX	17,536	413,516	198,987
Broward County Libraries Division, FL	16,889	439,962	221,310
Los Angeles Public Library, CA	15,874	333,988	160,895
Saint Louis County Library, MO	15,590	450,490	327,437

Are you and libraries right for each other?

There's no point in selling mice to an elephant. If after answering a few quick questions you determine that performing at libraries is not a good fit, then move on. Time is, as they say, money; don't waste your money or the librarian's time (or vice versa).

I assume (dangerous I know) that each performer in the group would like to make between $75 and $100 per performance (or more) at a show, and that there are between one and three people in your group. If your assumptions are different, please adjust accordingly.

Listed below are a few questions to determine if your program will be generally of interest to libraries before spending a great deal of time talking to librarians.

How many people are required to present your program?

How large is your band, dance troupe, or presentation crew? If a presentation requires more than four to five people then it is likely that working at libraries will not be cost effective. Large groups will quickly be priced out of the library market except for special events.

What is your minimum fee?

Realistically speaking, will your group work for $250 for an hour presentation? $200? $50? If your minimum fee is $600+ per show, then working in the library market on a regular basis will prove challenging. If you can comfortably perform for $300 a show, then continue reading. We will take a more in-depth look at pricing and pricing options later.

Is your performance family friendly?

If your performance were a movie, what would it be rated? G to PG13 is usually okay. R rated performances are a tough sell. Highly political or religious presentations, be they music, storytelling, or art are also a tough sell.

However, if you offer educational programs on hot topics – then you *may* have more luck in your efforts. Librarians like education and culture as well as entertainment. Remember – their goal is to bring more people to the library and increase those numbers I showed you earlier. Will your program do that?

Can you perform in small spaces?

For the purposes of this question a small space is defined as an eight-foot by four-foot space. That is the smallest performance space that I personally witnessed at a library. (Yes that's a tight space, and for some libraries, that's all they have available. Luckily that's an extreme example.) If your act requires a great deal of space it is, at the very least, important that you let the librarian know that ahead of time.

Are you able to perform to an audience of two?

It sounds like a silly question, but on occasion, no matter what you do, or what the library does to advertise, only two people show up to a presentation. It's always disappointing when things like this happen. That being said, are you able to do your presentation anyway? Are you able to accept this situation gracefully and be professional about it? This is important: if you make a bad impression, the librarian will never ask you back. If you make a good impression, it's considerably more likely that they will. Librarians are looking for groups that are flexible, and enthusiastic as well as polite and professional.

Does your presentation involve fire or dangerous substances?

No I'm not joking. Yes, this comes up sometimes. If your presentation involves fire or other dangerous materials, then it probably is not suited for regular library consumption. Most (not all) library presentations take place indoors in small spaces. Programs involving fire and dangerous substances may be a tough sell.

Do you enjoy being paid on time by friendly people?

Most people do. As long as you get your paperwork to them in a timely manner then libraries are excellent about paying on time. In six years of working with hundreds of libraries, only a handful didn't pay on time, and of that handful, none of them stiffed me on the check. The longest we had to wait was eight weeks, due to an incorrect address on a performer's payment form. (Side note: make sure to fill out the paperwork in a timely manner and with the correct information.)

If you were able to answer all of these questions successfully, then it is likely that your presentation is compatible with a library. Librarians like to provide a wide range of programs that expose their patrons to new ideas, new music, new performance styles, and new experiences, all while being fun and entertaining. As you work your way through this book, keep this in mind and craft ways to describe your program to fit those needs.

NOTES

NOTES

HOW TO FIND LIBRARIES

You can do this the easy way or the hard way. The hard way would be looking up the libraries individually, visiting their websites and searching out the contact information. I did that for a while. If it's for the occasional gig, it's not too bad, but if you're planning on performing at libraries full time, or as one of your primary venues, there is a much easier way. I found it entirely by accident, after many hours of searching for some sort of resource to make my job as an agent easier.

Public Schools and Public Libraries are, generally speaking, government institutions. And as government institutions, you can get their phone numbers, addresses and mailing addresses for free if you know how to do it. This does require the use of Microsoft Excel, or a program that will open an Excel spreadsheet.

The Microsoft Suite can be expensive, a free, open source alternative is LibreOffice. http://www.libreoffice.org/ I have not used this product, but it came highly recommended by one of my computer gurus.

Here's how to find libraries:

1. Visit the website for the Institute of Museum and Library Services (http://www.imls.gov/)

2. At the top, under the Research tab, select Data Collection, then Public Library Survey.

3. This will take you to a page called 'Public Libraries in the United States Survey'

4. Click on 'Search for Public Libraries.'

5. This will open a new tab or window with a search box.

   a. Here's where you have options. My preference was always to download an entire state at one time and do a more concentrated search once the information was in my possession, but you can search by state, by county, by area code etc. You will be downloading the file to store on your computer.

6. Fill in your search terms and click the search button on the right hand side.

   a. You may get a box that says 'Search Tip.' Click OK to continue with your search.

7. At the bottom of the search window you should see 'Download Excel File' in tiny letters, with an icon showing an Excel spreadsheet.

8. Click on Download Excel File

   a. Another box may pop up asking if you want to download the Excel File or a Zip file. Click Download the Excel File.

9. If a box asking if you want to open or save the document appears, select 'Open with Microsoft Excel' or whichever spreadsheet program your computer supports.

You should now have (depending on the state) a large spreadsheet. A good portion of the data can be deleted to make it more manageable.

You will want to keep the following columns:

a. **LIBNAME**
b. **LIBSYSNAME**
c. **STABR (State)**
d. **CITY**
e. **ADDRESS**
f. **CNTY**
g. **PHONE**
h. **ZIP**
i. You may also want to keep the columns associated with the mailing address. **(ADDRESS_M, CITY_M, ZIP_M)** everything else can be deleted.

You now have all of the main library contact information for each region or state you chose at your fingertips. As a bonus, you acquired it much more quickly than looking up the libraries individually. Time is money.

Another website that may be of use is http://www.publiclibraries.com. The information on this site is not as complete, but they frequently have links to the libraries' websites.

You've just received a large quantity of data. Now begins the process of sorting through what you actually want and need, and deciding what to get rid of. Don't worry about messing up your spreadsheet – you can always go download the data again if needed.

NOTES

PLANNING THE TOUR &
CONTACTING LIBRARIES

"I am always excited to work with presenters who aren't just good performers but who are organized on the back end. I put a lot of time and effort into library programs and it's wonderful to work with someone who is on the ball, communicates clearly and in a timely manner with me as needed, and generally doesn't leave me worrying about whether they'll have it together when they get here."

> Heather Backman
> Adult Services Librarian
> Hopkinton Public Library

Now it's time to contact the libraries, right? Wait just a second! Have you decided where you're going yet or how long you plan to be on the road? Contacting libraries (or any venue) costs either time or money or both. Before you start contacting libraries willy-nilly you need to plan where you want to tour, decide how long you will be on tour, decide what age group your presentations are aimed at, and have written program descriptions. All of these steps are outlined below.

There are two methods to deciding where to go, either one is valid, but they require different mindsets and methods. As a note, while running the agency I found that performers who tour over large regions, or nationally via car (or RV, or tour bus), are able to schedule more shows at libraries.

Option 1 – The Planner

You have a big gig already scheduled several months from now (preferably three to six months out). In this instance, get your map out, or better yet, get on Google or MapQuest and get directions between your current location and the location of your gig. Make a note of any cities along the route or within 30 miles of the route and cross-reference that with your list of libraries. Now you know which libraries you will contact.

Option 2 – The Organic

Decide which region of the country you want to tour, with no fixed destination in mind. This allows a wider 'net' when looking at libraries. Pick cities in the region that you would like to perform in and plan to stay a day or two in each.

A useful tool is a map-radius locator. You type in the name of a city, and how many miles (30 – 50 is usually good) and it shows you all of the cities and towns within that radius. These tools are available online for free, just do a search for map-radius locator.

When looking at the map, don't forget the smaller surrounding towns! Rural libraries can usually only schedule one or two programs a year but it is quite possible to perform at them every year, or every other year and build up a loyal fan base.

Okay – we've figured out which touring method you prefer, now we're going to contact the libraries right? Oops, not quite yet. How long do you plan to be on the road, and what are your tour dates? This is important for a few reasons:

1. How long can your sanity handle being on the road? This may not be something you discover

until you've done it a few times, so be willing to experiment with tour length. Some performers are fine being on the road year round, 100% of the time. Other performers can't fathom being away from home for longer than three weeks. Either way is fine, but it is important to know. If you can't handle being on the road for six weeks, don't plan a six-week tour.

2. It is important to know how long the tour will be so that you can roughly calculate expenses.

3. Knowing how long the tour will last and the dates you will be on the road allows you to tell librarians and other venues when you will be in their area. Knowing when you'll be there makes scheduling shows much easier.

We've figured out the when, the where, and the how long, now do you know what age group you want to perform for? I promise, we'll contact the libraries soon.

Libraries generally offer programing for Children, Teens, Adults, Seniors (age 65+), and Family. It's helpful to know which area your performance falls into before you have someone on the phone. If you already know what age group your performance is best suited for, skip the next several paragraphs.

Libraries break down the age groups roughly as follows:

1. **Ages 0-12: Children**. This is a huge range, and frequently programs are broken down further by age group, but usually the same person is in charge of all programs for this grouping. To determine if a program will be entertaining for children ask a few questions, and get feedback from your peers.

    a. Will children enjoy my program?

        i. Test it out. Borrow your neighbor's kids (with permission of course!) have a small get together and see if you can keep a group of kids (more than 4 or 5) entertained with your music or storytelling for an hour.

    b. Will adults enjoy my program?

        i. If both children and adults will enjoy your program, it's not a children's program, it's a Family program. MOST adults will not willingly sit through a children's program unless their child is in attendance.

    c. What children's programs have I seen?

        i. If the answer is none – take a few moments to look through YouTube at puppet shows, storytellers, and children's musicians. What do they all have in common? They engage directly with the children and keep them <u>actively</u> involved.

    d. Do I already have a children's book, CD or DVD on the market?

        i. Yes, you are a children's entertainer.

2. **Ages 13-18: Teens**. Many libraries don't offer teen programing, but those that do are always thrilled to find a group or presenter that specializes in teenagers. Libraries that have programing specifically for teens are more often found in large cities and suburbs surrounding those cities. Teen programs can range from writing & music workshops and concerts to Hunger Games style Live Action Role Playing games.

3. **Ages 19-64: Adults.** Many libraries have monthly programs for adults such as concert series, lecture series, or experiential learning. The variety of programs for adults is endless.

4. **Ages 65+: Seniors.** In most cases programing for seniors will be housed under programing for Adults, but occasionally there are programs that are restricted to this age group. (As in, don't bring your small children unless they are exceptionally well behaved.)

5. **Family Programs.** Quite a few libraries like to host programs for the whole family. Programs that are suitable for all age ranges, and can genuinely keep both children and adults interested would fall into this group.

Decide which group (or groups) your presentation falls into. Be honest! If a performance isn't designed to keep 200 five year olds entertained for an hour, don't bill yourself as a children's performer. If your performance IS designed exclusively for children, don't bill yourself as a family or adult performer. If you are unsure, talk to someone who has seen your presentation and get his or her feedback.

The Dangers of Misrepresenting – An Example

David (not his actual name) is an excellent folk musician who has been performing for 20 years or more as a sideline business. When he retired from his day job (also in the music industry) he decided to tour more and try to make a go of being a full time musician. He had been performing for nearly two decades, and like many experienced professionals came to us wanting a little extra boost to his bookings, and a little extra help on the booking side of things. When I spoke with him about the types of shows he performed, he had a program specifically for Seniors and several more that classified as Family programs. We marketed him for several months with limited success.

David heard that Children's programing was the place to be. He came back to me and said that he felt his Family program could be marketed specifically as a Children's program. After much discussion on the matter, I agreed that we could try it. We booked him into a library system for four performances over two days for the library's summer reading program. The shows came and went, and he seemed very pleased. His report to us was glowing – he definitely wanted to go back. As was standard practice for the agency, we contacted the library after the performance to check in with the librarian, solicit a letter of recommendation for David, and to see about follow up bookings.

I received no response for several months (not that unusual, as summer is the busiest time for libraries). When I contacted the librarian about potentially booking David in for another show I still didn't receive a response. As chance would have it, I ran into her at a library conference and managed to sit down for a chat. When I brought up David she gave me a pained look and admitted that she had been avoiding my emails and calls. David, she said, seemed to be a fine performer, but his program had not at all been suited to children, it had not kept them engaged, and because of this she couldn't recommend him, and wouldn't bring him back to the library. She felt mislead by his program descriptions and that her patrons had not been well served. She hadn't known how to say it politely, and so had been avoiding me instead.

David did a disservice to himself, wanting to be billed as a children's performer without having an actual children's presentation prepared, and the agency did a disservice to David by agreeing to book him as a children's performer when he clearly wasn't. Hopefully this example will keep you from making the same mistake. You might get away with it once or twice, but librarians do talk to each other and word will get around.

Calling the library

Now that you've determined what age group your presentation is best suited for, we'll discuss who to talk to at the library. The vast majority of librarians in charge of programs work between the hours of ten a.m. and six p.m.

There are of course outliers, but those hours are the most profitable for actually getting in touch with people.

Your call will be answered by the front desk – your best bet is to first ask, **"Who is in charge of programing for the library?"** either they will ask you "Children's or Adult's?" or you will get a blank silence at the other end of the line. Not all libraries do programing, and not all front desk people know the answers. Sometimes explaining what you mean by programing is the best course.

If you are getting the blank silence treatment from the front desk, ask to be transferred either to the Children's librarian (Children's & sometimes Teen programs), the Reference Desk (Adult & Senior programs), or the Library Director (person who knows everything about the library but who is generally very busy). Be careful about contacting the general library email address, it probably won't get to the right person, and be careful about contacting the Director.

Tom Cooper, Director of the Webster Groves Public Library has this to say:

The director is very often the worst person to speak with about booking a performance. Try to talk with Children's or Adult Services Librarians, who are more likely to be planning these things. As a director, I can't tell you how many times I've had a card or a flyer from a performer sitting on my desk for weeks before finally discarding it because it was just clutter to me.

When you find the person in charge of booking programs, get their name, direct phone number and email address. Verify the spelling with them! There's nothing more frustrating than getting an email address and discovering after you've hung up that it's spelled incorrectly.

A typical conversation might go like this:
You: "Hi! My name is _____. I'm with [**insert**

your group name here]. We're a [**group type i.e. folk music duo, juggling act, science education group**]. We'll be travelling through your area [**insert dates here**] and wanted to see if you would be interested in having us perform at your library."

Librarian: "I've never heard of you. Do you have a website?"

You: "Yes! Our web address is [**insert your website**] and I'd be happy to email you some information as well. Can I get your email address?"

Librarian: "Sure, my email address is xxxxx@library.tx.us"

You: "Great! I'll email that information over right away. When would be a good time to follow up with you?"

Librarian: "Check back with me in a couple of weeks, that's when I'll be working on booking our [fall, spring, summer, winter] programing."

You: "Would you prefer an email follow up, or a phone call?"

Occasionally you will run across librarians who simply don't want to hear what you have to say. Typical responses in those cases are 'We don't do programs.' Or 'We can't afford you (whether you've given them a price or not).' Don't beat your head against a brick wall – if they brush you off, thank them for their time and make a note not to call them again for a year or so.

Once you get off the phone, <u>immediately email the information they requested</u>. Be sure to include your name, website, phone number and email address in the signature line of the email. Most email programs will have an option to set this up so that you don't have to type it every time.

It is okay to have a form email/letter that you send, just make sure to add in the person's name in the right places. A form email for a follow up to a phone call might look like this:

Dear Tammy,

Thank you for taking the time to speak with me this afternoon. My group, Sampson and Delilah Juggling, will be touring through your area June 5-7, 2016. You can find out more about the group on our website at www.[insertwebaddresshere].com

Attached please find a listing of the different programs we offer, along with descriptions and recommended age groups for each.

If you have any questions, or would like to schedule a performance, please contact me at performer@emailaddresshere.com or by phone at (123) 303-4567.

I look forward to hearing from you soon.

[Your Name]
Phone: (123) 555-4567
Email: performer@emailaddresshere.com
Website: www.[insertwebaddresshere].com

One of the things you will want to include when you send this message is one or two different program descriptions that accurately describe what it is that you do. Each program should have a separate description. Below is a sample, and a list of what should be included.

Written Program Descriptions

One of the most useful things to have in your arsenal of promotional materials is a coherent, well written description of your program. A program description should include:

- A catchy title that is descriptive of the program
- The age group the program is intended for
- The length of the program
- If the program meets any of the Academic Standards for a particular state. (This is more important for performing at schools, but is still useful for libraries.)
- An interesting, informative blurb about the program that will encourage venues to choose this program.

Each program should have its own description. For example, if a historical impersonator does a program with Benjamin Franklin, and another with Mark Twain, each would get their own description. The same would be true for a musician that offers a Family program on Celtic music, and a Children's program on how to play the recorder.

Here is a sample program description:

Instrument Education Concert for children of all ages: material to be selected based on maturity/age level:

About the group

As a duo, Bettman & Halpin are fast earning a reputation for hypnotizing performances filled with irresistible lyrics, transcendent harmonies and roof-raising instrumentals. Their music creates a fully acoustic, delightfully eclectic sound far greater than the sum of its parts: taking the listener from up-tempo down home fiddlin', to soulful sorrowful ballads, to super hooky folk/pop with catchy melodies and lyrics that will stick with you long after the concert is over.

About the program

For this program Bettman & Halpin perform a short concert (30 – 45 min) for children's groups, with a question and answer session afterwards. This is approximately a one hour program. During the concert they take some time in between songs to talk about their instruments, how they started writing music, the history of folk and bluegrass music etc. and answer questions from the participants as they arise.

Academic Standards

This program meets and supports the following Academic Standards in the state of Colorado for grades 9-12:

- Theory of Music: Classification by genre, style, historical period, or culture.
- Aesthetic Valuation of Music:
  - Practice of appropriate behavior during cultural activities.
- Knowledge of available musical opportunities for continued musical growth and professional development.

Contact information

To find out about more of our programs, or schedule a performance please visit our website at www.[insertwebaddresshere].com or give us a call at (123) 555-4567.

Your contact information should be clearly visible on every document you send out.

Promotional Mailings to Libraries

Many established performers have gotten into the routine of mailing out pre-printed postcards or flyers to all of the schools and libraries in the areas where they would like to tour. This method has both good points and bad points:

Good:

1. It generates name recognition for the group.
2. Flyers and postcards can contain an excellent sales pitch.
3. It will usually generate a booking or two.

Bad:

1. Postal rates continue to rise, and between the cost of printing the flyers and mailing them, it can get expensive very quickly.
2. Most flyers and postcards will immediately find their way to the nearest trashcan.
3. Mis-addressed flyers and postcards don't reach their intended recipients AND cost money.

Most librarians polled for this book said that they would prefer an email to a postcard, but that more information on a group was better, no matter how it got to them. Use your judgment about whether the expense of sending postcards out is worth it.

Postcards, if they are being sent out, should at a minimum include what you do, contact information, and website. Schools of thought vary on including prices on mailings. And for the love of everything holy <u>make sure you proofread it!</u> There is nothing more embarrassing than printing up and sending out advertisements with typos. If you aren't good at proofreading, have a friend look at it for you.

Make sure that every venue that gets a mailed card gets a follow up call the next week.

Follow up calls and emails

It is unlikely that the library will book a show on first contact. This is true for most venues and so it is important to make follow up calls in a timely manner. If someone has given a specific time frame on when to get back in touch, make sure that you follow up within that period of time. If they did not give a time frame, follow up approximately one week later. The most reliable way to keep track of this (and to remind yourself to follow up) is to use a calendar, either electronic or good old-fashioned paper.

Google has a free online calendar that is accessible from just about any Internet enabled electronic device. Online calendars are useful because they allow putting quite a bit of information (such as names, phone numbers and locations) in the event notes when reminders are set up to call people. The downfall of course is that occasionally electronic devices and services fail and there is a slight risk of losing all of your information.

On average it will take five follow up phone calls or emails to a library before they give an answer – three of those will probably involve leaving messages for the librarian. Unlike many jobs, librarians don't spend a lot of time sitting at their desk, so it can be hard to get in touch with them. Sending emails early in the morning so that messages are waiting for them when they get to work will sometimes elicit a faster response.

Reminder: No more than one follow up message per week unless they request otherwise. Polite persistence is the name of the game.

NOTES

BOOKING TRENDS

As you work at libraries more, you will find certain things to be true.

- ❖ The more you work at libraries, the easier it is to work at libraries.
  - o Librarians talk to one another quite a bit. Mentioning other libraries where you have performed, particularly in the same geographic area, can assist in scheduling future shows.
  - o Keep a reference list (with names and contact information) of libraries where your program went really well. Give this out to librarians that ask for references.
- ❖ The farther afield you roam from home base, the easier it is to schedule library programs. Touring nationally you will have more options than if you tour regionally. Touring regionally will give you more options than if you stay in one state.
- ❖ There is ebb and flow to when libraries schedule shows. Certain trends are nationwide, and some are regional. The months of December, January, February and March are when most of the scheduling for June,

July and August is accomplished nationwide. Making booking phone calls during the month of August is, for most of the country, an effort in futility. All of the librarians are out on vacation, or collapsed in the back of the library with a pitcher of margaritas going, "Thank God Summer Reading is Over." Most other times of the year booking for programing is done in the quarter prior.

❖ Summer Reading usually runs June – July except in New York. In New York Summer Reading is in August.

❖ Summer Reading is the goldmine/jackpot of a performer's year if they start planning early enough. This is true everywhere except Florida. In Florida they prefer fall and winter bookings. (Though they do have a Summer Reading program, so contacting them is not useless.)

❖ Start trying to book Summer Reading programs in November of the year prior. Not all libraries schedule this far out, but many of them do. Booking for Summer Reading runs approximately from November of the previous year through April of the same year. (i.e. if you are booking shows for Summer Reading 2016 you should start making calls to librarians in November of 2015.) Jean Hatfield, Branch Manager of the Wichita Public Library has this to say:

> *Keep in mind when you're trying to schedule shows, some libraries must turn in their program plans months in advance, so waiting until spring to send information about the summer program may be too late.*

❖ Throughout most of the country Summer Reading follows a theme. This theme is determined by the Collaborative Summer Library Program organization. They announce themes up to three years in advance. Performers that tailor their program to the specific themes and advertise well in advance will find themselves with more bookings.

❖ Libraries that do large block bookings (four or more shows for one performer) usually work eight months to a year out.

❖ Certain parts of the country tend to have fewer programing opportunities at libraries.

    o Because of a lack of funding the southeastern United States (Louisiana, Mississippi, Alabama, and Arkansas in particular) is a particularly difficult area to schedule shows at libraries. Hopefully that will improve.

    o Utah and Nevada outside the main cities are challenging (but not impossible) because of the sparse population. North Dakota faces a similar challenge.

    o Alaska and Hawaii are difficult to schedule because of the geographic challenges, but Hawaii, last I checked, had a thriving library system. They tend to schedule farther out (eight months to a year in advance).

❖ Libraries that host concert series are particularly valuable for musicians. There are quite a few libraries that do monthly or seasonal concert series. Two of the most popular in the West are the Thousand Oaks concert series in California, and the Fort Stockton Public Library in west Texas, but there are <u>many</u> out there.

❖ There are three major national library conferences every year – the Annual Library Association Conference, the ALA Midwinter Conference, and the Public Library Association Conference. During these conferences, half the librarians you try to contact will be out of the office, and a quarter of the librarians you do get in touch with will be grumpy that they are not at the conference.

    o Each conference has a Twitter #hashtag and a huge number of librarians are on Twitter. Find out what the hashtag is, and send a few tweets out during the conference to the librarians there. Do not spam the hashtag – it won't do your reputation any good.

- A sample tweet might look something like this: Children's #librarians we couldn't be at #ALAmidwinter2014 to show off our new storytime, but you can see a sample at [www.insertwebaddresshere.com]

o If any one of the conferences is in a city near you (they move around yearly) get a pass to the vendor floor – it's cheaper than a conference pass, a lot of fun, and will give you a chance to see how other people advertise to libraries. It is expensive to get a booth (think $2000+) so analyze your finances carefully before taking that particular plunge.

❖ Most states have a yearly State Library Association conference. These are considerably cheaper to attend and the price for a vendor booth is less prohibitive (think $100-$400 except Texas and California). This also allows you to target your touring regions more specifically and collect email addresses and phone numbers of librarians interested in programing.

Elizabeth vonTauffkirchen, Director of Children's Services at the Pine River Library had this to say:

Be visible. Getting your face and PR materials out into the library community is vitally important. If we don't know about you, we can't book you.

There are thousands of librarians on Twitter. Learn how to use Twitter, follow librarians (not libraries) and announce where you are planning to tour using the hashtag #librarians #library or #summerreading. Announce when you book a show in an area. Encourage librarians to visit your website via Twitter as well.

NOTES

NOTES

MAILING LISTS

At first glance this section may not seem directly related to actually booking and scheduling shows, but it is, and in fact it is a very large part of booking repeat shows. Email lists are crucial to performers and presenters. If you don't have one yet, it's important to start one. In fact, start two.

Email Mailing List 1 – For the Fans

As a performer you should have a mailing list for your fans – this will let you communicate with your fans about when and where you are performing, and when you have new products out (CD's, T-shirts, DVD's, YouTube Videos etc.) Giving special deals and sales to those fans smart enough to be on your list is an incentive for them to buy more stuff.

For a large and geographically diverse mailing list, it is a good idea to segment it by state so that you're not notifying people in New York that you have a show in Los Angeles. Sending out non-relevant emails will cause people to drop off the mailing list faster than anything else.

How often should you email fans? No more than once a week, no less than once a month. Stay in front of the fans. Make sure to tell them about upcoming gigs, new releases, places they can buy your products, and any good press you've received.

How do you get fans on your mailing list? It is reasonably easy to set up a link for fans to sign up on your website, using a variety of mailing list services. It is also a good idea to set out a piece of paper for fans to write their email addresses down at gigs. (You can add them to the mailing list manually later.)

Email Mailing List 2 – For the Venues

One of the first things we asked for from the librarian was their email address. Keep a separate mailing list just for library and school venues. Make sure you keep track of names, states and, if you do both children's and adult's programing, what kind of programs that person focuses on. Three to six months before you travel to a region, start emailing your venue mailing list with your proposed dates, program descriptions, and any new programs that you have developed. Don't forget to include any discounts you may offer for groups that book early, or that book multiple programs.

As an agent, fully twenty-five to thirty-five percent of my repeat bookings for groups came from sending out an email to an area where they had performed before – the work of maybe ten minutes. Successful mailing lists can take years to build, but they are worth maintaining and in the long run will save you time and money.

The CANSPAM act of 2003

Reminder – the CANSPAM act of 2003 requires that you include certain identifiers in any email that you send out to a mailing list for commercial purposes. The Bureau of Consumer Protection website lists the following as the main requirements:

    1. Don't use false or misleading header

information. – The 'From', 'To' and 'Reply-to' fields need to lead back to you.

2. Don't use deceptive subject lines.

3. Identify the message as an ad. – You can say this in the fine print at the bottom and be covered.

4. Tell recipients where you're located – Per the website: "Your message must include your valid physical postal address. This can be your current street address, a post office box you've registered with the U.S. Postal Service, or a private mailbox you've registered with a commercial mail receiving agency established under Postal Service regulations."

5. Tell recipients how to opt out of receiving future email from you. – Include unsubscribe instructions, or a link in the footer of your email.

6. Honor opt-out requests promptly.

7. Monitor what others are doing on your behalf. – If you have someone (a volunteer, employee, or third party service) sending out emails for you make sure you know what they're sending out.

Reputable mailing list services:

❖ Constant Contact - their service price is based on how many people are on the mailing list, not how many emails are sent out, but a mailing list of around 2,500 costs approximately $35 a month. They are reliable and have excellent metrics for tracking how many people open emails and click on links. Their tutorials and initial setup will help comply with the CANSPAM act. Emails can be scheduled to send at specific times, and it is possible to set up welcome emails for people that join the list. Everything is done online, so editing emails can be cumbersome if your Internet connection is slow.

❖ Direct Mail – This service is primarily for Mac users. Users buy credits and are charged per email sent (recommended), or can send emails out through their own mail server (not recommended). The more credits purchased at a time, the less they cost per email. Sending fewer than 50 emails a month is free. Graphic emails are built off-line but require an Internet connection to send. The user interface can be difficult to use and has a bit of a learning curve, but it is reasonably cost effective if you're not sending out a lot of emails.

❖ Mail Chimp – I myself have not used this service, but a number of musicians and other small businesses that I have worked with over the years have recommended them.

❖ Other services you can check out include:
  o YMLP (Your Mailing List Provider) https://www.ymlp.com
  o Benchmark Mail http://www.benchmarkemail.com/
  o Mad Mimi https://www.madmimi.com

There are countless other services like these out there – the important thing to remember is that 1) You need a mailing list 2) A third-party service to manage the mailing list is needed (and desirable for your sanity) 3) Follow the CANSPAM guidelines or your emails will get blacklisted and will not get to fans.

NOTES

NOTES

PRICING

The librarian calls you back and says, "Your program looks really interesting, what are your fees?" Instead of floundering for an answer, or underselling yourself, (a common problem among creative types) know what your options are in advance.

The Sliding Scale Fee

One way to address this question is to offer a sliding scale fee using different scales for different types of venues. For libraries a reasonable sliding scale for professional performers is usually $300-$600 for a duo, modify the numbers slightly up or down for a solo performer, or a trio etc.

There are a number of things to keep in mind when using a sliding scale fee.

1. Make sure the lower number on the scale is a price you're willing to perform for, and is slightly higher than the lowest amount you're *actually* willing to perform for. (Leave some negotiating room in case you need it.)

2. When using a sliding scale fee model there is very little negotiation – any number the venue names

on the scale should be fine. This means two things:

    a. You will never perform at a library for less than the lowest number on the scale

    b. You can estimate, based on how many library bookings you average a year and the lowest fee, how much money you can expect to make over a given period of time. (For example: Last year you performed 30 library gigs at $300 each, equaling $9,000 in gig fees.)

3. Using a sliding scale fee does make negotiating multiple bookings at the same library more difficult to price, as many venues expect a discount. The key is to be flexible and know what your absolute minimum is per show.

A sample conversation might sound something like this:

Venue: How much do you charge?

You: My group works on a sliding scale fee for libraries of $300-$600 plus lodging. You can pick your own price anywhere within that range, whatever you think is fair and works best with your budget.

Venue: So... it's the same show no matter the price?

You: Yes! We ask that libraries that can pay a little more do so voluntarily so that we can still continue to perform for libraries that can't pay quite as much. But you get the same high quality show either way.

Most groups that I worked with were concerned that they would always receive the lowest price quoted. What we found after doing this for a number of years is that more often than not during good budget years libraries pay more, and during lean budget years they pay less. In our last year of operations, using this model, shows were averaging around $400 - $450 per show.

The Fixed Price Model

The alternative to a sliding scale model is a fixed price model. This model is fairly self-explanatory – decide what price to charge and quote that. Sticking between $200-$600 for a one hour show is still going to land in about the right spot (again, based on how many people are in the group.)

Benefits of a fixed price model include:

1. Having one price to quote will help avoid confusion and require less explanation.
2. The fixed price model allows the ability to offer set discounts for multiple performances on the same day.

The downside to the fixed price model is that if the price is substantially higher than what the library can afford they will usually decline to hire you, even if you would have been willing to drop your price to accommodate them.

A sample conversation might go like this:

Venue: How much do you charge?

You: It depends a little bit on what you want. We charge $450 for a one hour concert plus lodging. If you schedule us for two performances in the same day it's $450 for the first performance and $275 for the second. That's a discount of $175.

Venue: We can't afford that much. Is there any way you could do a show for around $300?

This is either where the negotiating begins, or where they accept or don't accept your price. Know in advance what your absolute lowest price is, this will give you some leeway in negotiations.

Think about these things in advance and decide which pricing model to use. If you're not certain, try both models out – just do it in different regions. Offering one library a fixed price, and the library just down the road a sliding scale fee is not a good idea. They will find out and one of them will be unhappy. They do talk to each other.

Thinking Beyond Money

As you are negotiating your fee, don't forget to ask about the extras:

❖ Do you need a hotel room for the night?

❖ Do you need mileage covered? (It's unlikely they will cover airfare.)

❖ Does your performance use expendable materials? (Some science programs for example.)

❖ Is the library planning on providing the equipment, or do you need to provide your own? (It's a good idea to provide your own if you can, as equipment provided by libraries is frequently heavily used and may not be the best quality.)

❖ Is it okay to sell CD's or other products at the library? Most libraries are okay with selling product after the show, but it's a good idea to check. Some libraries require that you fill out tax documents before selling product, and some libraries don't allow it at all.

At the same time, as you ponder what else you need to add in to your negotiations remember, Libraries are not big venues, they may not be able to provide everything you need.

Per Joan Dorfman, the Reference Librarian at the Bloomfield Public Library:

Inform the librarian (booking the show) as early as possible if you have any special needs for the performance. Some [performers] need a podium, others a certain type of chair, some need a projector, smartboard, bottles of water, some need help unloading their equipment, some need a parking space close to the door, some need the chairs set up in a certain configuration, some need a private dressing area, etc.

The more advance notice you can give on items you may need, the more likely it is you will get them. Ideally make sure they're written in to the contract.

NOTES

NOTES

Touring Basics, Promoting &

Keeping Your Sanity on the Road

CONTRACTS, COMPUTERS & OTHER DOCUMENTS

If you're an experienced performer you already know this. <u>Always get it in writing.</u> Libraries are wonderful to work with, but it's still a good idea to cover your bases. Having a contract in writing gives recourse in the event that something goes wrong. As an example, sometimes things get double booked by accident, someone quits or gets fired and hasn't told anyone they booked you, or you get sick, or the library forgets you're coming. (Yes, it happens.)

In this particular regard, working with libraries can be both wonderful and frustrating. In most cases libraries are happy to sign a contract if provided one. Occasionally they have one of their own that they require performers to sign. Very occasionally they want it notarized and signed in triplicate.

The basic elements to include in a contract:
1. Date, time, and location of the performance
2. Length of the presentation
3. Performer's name/Group Name

4. Payment terms, including price, when the presenter will be paid, and who the check should be made out to.
5. What the performer is providing (for example: 1 hour performance titled: XXXX)
6. What the venue is providing (for example: sound equipment, puppet theater, projector, stage etc.)
7. What will each group do to promote the show? An example: Artist will promote the performance by adding the show to their online calendar, and notifying fans by email and social media. Venue will promote the show by putting up posters, flyers, notifying local papers, and adding the event to their online calendar.
8. What happens if the performance is cancelled, or the performer doesn't show up? Make sure this is explicitly stated.
9. A place for both parties to sign the contract.

Joan Dorfman, Reference Librarian for the Bloomfield Public Library has this to say:

A performer should have a list prepared of what they will need for the performance. Then they can send it out to the library to have it checked off, signed and returned (if they want). Many arguments start because of a misunderstanding of what the performers need.

Here are two separate sample contracts. Feel free to use them in whole or in part, and modify them to suit your needs. You can also download them on my website at www.jessicabrawner.com

LETTER OF AGREEMENT

This agreement is between [PERFORMER] and [VENUE]. On [DATE] [PERFORMER] will perform at [VENUE] from [BLOCK OF TIME]

Admission will be $_____. [PERFORMER]will be paid $_____ for presentation. **The presentation fee will be paid upon completion of the performance unless prior arrangements have been made.**

Payment should be made out to [PERFORMER].

The [VENUE] will advertise by putting out flyers, and through email and/or online calendars as is appropriate.

[PERFORMER] will advertise by listing performance on calendars, websites, Press Releases etc.

[PERFORMER] will be allowed to sell CDs, T-shirts and other items related to the program at the [VENUE].

ARTIST REQUIREMENTS

List anything you need the venue to provide. Items might include bottled water, digital projector, electrical outlets, music stands, podium, basically anything that you can't provide yourself. Remember, libraries can't usually provide much, but it ALWAYS helps to ask in advance. Asking when you show up and not in advance is a recipe for disaster.

[PERFORMER] will ensure performance barring injury, illness, death and acts of God. [VENUE] will provide performance space barring all of the above. [VENUE] will be liable for payment if [PERFORMER] is not informed of schedule changes within 5 business days of the performance. [PERFORMER] will notify [VENUE] of any and all changes as soon as information is available. [PERFORMER] will do their best to notify [VENUE] of any cancellation with at least 48 hours notice if possible. If [PERFORMER] is unable to perform for reasons cause by or relating to themselves [VENUE] will NOT be required to pay for the performance.

[PERFORMER] will arrive 1 to 1.5 hours before the performance to prepare the performance space.

By signing below both parties are in agreement. Any and all disputes will be handled by professional mediation if necessary.

_____   _____

[PERFORMER] [DATE]   [VENUE] [DATE]

A simple version could look something like this:

PERFORMER NAME
ADDRESS
PHONE

Performer:_____

Name of Act: (if

applicable)_____

Venue address:_____

City:_____ State_____ Zip_____

Phone:_____

Contact Person:_____

Email Address:_____

****

Compensation:

[VENUE] will pay [PERFORMER] $_____ for
the following performance :

List a brief description of the performance including:

Performance Title:_____

Length of Performance: _____

Number of performances per day:_____

Requested performance dates: _____

Performance fee will be paid at the time of the
performance.

[VENUE REPRESENTATIVE]   [DATE]

[PERFORMER REPRESENTATIVE]   [DATE]

Electronic vs. Paper

Being on the road I always found it easier to do things electronically – email them a copy of the contract, have them scan and email a signed copy of it back to me, no need for filing cabinets and keeping track of bits of paper. (This was also handy when my house burned down; I didn't lose much of my business information, and was able to continue with only a few small hitches.) If you tour regularly, I recommend learning to use the electronic tools at your disposal. They will save you time, money, and headaches once you learn how to use them.

A sample electronic filing system might look like this:

Folder 1: Group Name

  Folder 2: Booking Information

    Folder 3: 2014 (Information for gigs happening in that year. Each year, create a new folder.)

      Folder 4: 2014 10 3 (Cleveland OH) (Year, month, day, city, state) Organizing it this way means that everything in Folder 3 will show up in order by date. Instead of the city and state you could put in the venue name if that would be helpful to you. Put everything related to the gig in this folder – contracts, press releases, reimbursements or tax forms that the library may send.

Other useful folders

Folder 2: Press Materials

  Folder 3: Press Photos – Professional photos of you and/or your group suitable for publication in print and online. Press photos should be at a minimum 2MB in size.

  Folder 3: Press Releases – Have a standard press release written up that you can edit to include the venue's name and the performance time/location.

  Folder 3: Letters of Recommendation – When you get letters of recommendation you will want to keep the originals in a safe place. You will also want to store electronic copies on your computer so that you can send them at a moment's notice. I recommend investing in a decent scanner or all in one printer/scanner/fax machine to keep at home. (All in one printer/scanner/fax machines are a great business tool, but much too big to bring on the road!) Scan your letters of recommendation as you get them.

Folder 2: Tax and Accounting Forms –store your W9, an invoice template, a blank contract, and any other forms that you use on a regular basis, or that you will need to send to the venue in this folder.

Folder 2: Contact and Mailing Lists – keep a spreadsheet backup of your contacts and/or your mailing lists.

NOTES

PROMOTING THE SHOW

Show promotion and libraries can be very hit or miss. Some libraries do a fantastic job promoting, and when you arrive in town you will see posters or flyers all over town advertising your show. Some libraries assume people are psychic and will simply know that something is going on at the library. And sometimes, no matter what you do, people still don't show up to the performance due to weather, the local football schedule, the county fair, or any number of other things.

Posters and Flyers

It has become more common for libraries to have someone in-house that can design a flyer for the show, however it's still a good idea to have one of your own. While fancy graphic design programs are nice when you are designing promotional materials, they are expensive, require learning the programs, and are not strictly necessary. It is entirely possible to design a respectable flyer or using just Microsoft Word. Alternatively you can of course pay someone else to do it and save yourself the headache.

You are a brand name. Flyers help promote your brand, and branding yourself means that people get the same message over and over again and are more likely to remember you. Think about this as you design a poster. You can't force the library to use your materials, (nor should you try to) but frequently they are happy to do so if provided one.

Mailing Lists

You have a mailing list; use it. Send an email to fans two weeks before you have a show in their area giving them the details, (or if you have several shows in the area, list all of them) then send a second email the day before the show reminding them. Many of the mailing list programs will allow you to schedule your emails to go out at specific times, so spend a day (or half a day) and set up all of the emails that you'll need for a month, and then forget about it until the next month.

For the forgetful, set up an email reminder telling you that there's a show coming up, and what the details are. It may seem silly, but if it keeps you from missing a performance, even once, then it is worth it.

Online Calendars

There are about a million online events calendars out there. Okay so I just made that number up, but that's what it feels like when you start adding shows to all of them. This is another case of work smarter not harder.

Artist Data is a service that was acquired by Sonic Bids a few years ago. It is primarily for musicians, though it can be used for other presenters. It is free to use, and hooks into many of the popular electronic calendars and services. They have a calendar that is easy to add to your website that will update automatically when you add the show under your login. (It's not pretty, but it does work, and it's easy.) It will also post to Facebook and Twitter automatically, reminding fans that you have a show coming up.

Go to www.artistdata.com and set up an account. News outlets prefer to receive information about shows more than twenty-one days in advance to give them time to add it to their print and online outlets. Every time you schedule a new show, or at least once every two weeks or so, go and add your shows to your profile. Artist Data will then notify a variety of different outlets, and your work is done for you.

Social Media

Between Facebook, Twitter, Pintrest, LinkedIn, Ello, and any number of other things, it's hard to know how to manage it all. Social Media and the uses thereof have been topics of much longer books that this one. In the vein of Artist Data, HootSuite will allow you to update most of your social media outlets with only one stop. It will also allow you to schedule posts in advance and track which posts get the most clicks. There is both a paid and a free version. I highly recommend http://www.hootsuite.com

Remember, while libraries may not be the most prestigious venues, they can be your bread and butter. If you bring in two hundred patrons and fans to a library that usually only gets fifty, they are almost guaranteed to bring you back again. **Promote the shows just like you would for any other venue.**

NOTES

GETTING PAID

Libraries pay in one of three ways – either, they mail a check before the show, they hand the performer a check at the show, or they mail the check after the show. How you're getting paid should be specified in your contract so that you know in advance.

Getting Paid Before the Show

I can't recommend this method. If the check is mailed to before the show, the money goes into your account in advance, which is nice, but then if the show is cancelled for any reason, you are responsible for paying that money back to the library. Most entertainers, most people in fact, spend money as soon as it comes in, which can leave you in a precarious position if the show is canceled.

Getting Paid at the Show

This is by far the most common method – just don't forget to pick up the check! Librarians are humans too, some of them are scatterbrained, and if you don't ask for the check they might forget to hand it to you. When on tour, it's a good idea to have a bank bag, or some specific place that you put checks. Not all banks are available all over the United States, and you may not be able to deposit the check immediately. Alternatively, if you bank at a credit union, many credit unions participate in the National Shared Branch Network. This network allows credit union members to deposit checks at a variety of locations that are affiliated with their credit union, and the money will still show up in their account. It's magic!

Getting Paid After the Show

Some libraries, because they are housed under the local government, or for a variety of other reasons, must mail the check after the performance. Frequently in these instances, because of their accounting procedures, this can take six to eight weeks. On the up-side, in six years of working with hundreds of libraries, I've never had a library not pay. On the down side, waiting for the check is no fun. Usually when they have to mail the check after the performance there is also a lot of additional paperwork. Make sure that the paperwork is filled out and returned it in a timely manner. Neglecting your paperwork can delay your check.

THE SHOW

"When you perform at a library, there may not be a big audience, there may be too big of an audience, they may not all be the right age - please be flexible in your preparations!"

Jean Hatfield
Branch Manager
Wichita Public Library

Call a few days before your program to verify the details with the librarian, and find out who to talk to the day of the show. The person that organized the show may not even be in the building during your performance. If you want someone to do an introduction, email the coordinator a bio, or better yet a short introduction blurb that they can read off directly.

The day of the performance show up between a half hour and an hour in advance of the program (or earlier if you need more time to set up). Library patrons frequently show up 30 minutes before an event is scheduled to start, and they can be impatient and grumpy if a performer is late. Be on time.

Being on time (30-60 minutes before the show) gives you the opportunity to set up in a relaxed manner, meet the librarian, check out the room, and see if the setup is to your liking. This also gives a time cushion in case there's traffic, car trouble, or in case the library forgets you're coming. (Yes, this does happen sometimes.)

Sue Ridnour, the Director of Library Services at the Flower Mound Public Library had this to say:

Program coordinators are going to have a heart attack if you run in five minutes before the show is scheduled to start! They understand that you have set up your show many times and have it timed down to the second, but if starting time details aren't specifically covered in the contract, they should be discussed informally before the performance.

I can't tell you how to do your program. Do it to the best of your ability. Act in a professional manner; be friendly and courteous. Arrange with the library to have a staff member in attendance at all times if possible so that there is someone available to deal with unruly patrons, or other emergencies if they come up during your performance.

<u>At the END of the presentation,</u> remind the audience about your website, Facebook Page, Mailing List, Patreon Account or any other social media and that you have product for sale. Don't forget to thank the library, and any sponsors that helped them pay for the show. Donating a copy of your CD, book or other product to the library is guaranteed to generate goodwill. Make an effort to end on time. One of the biggest complaints that I saw consistently was shows that either started late or ran over their allotted time.

As a side note, this shouldn't need to be said, but as a few librarians mentioned it, I will too. <u>Do not complain about the venue from the stage</u>. If something goes wrong, deal with it either before or after the show with the person that organized the event. Do not be a Diva, and do not vent from stage, it is unprofessional in the extreme.

Selling Product at the Show

Having product to sell is an excellent boost to your income. Telling people at the end of your show that you have product available for purchase is a great idea. Telling them five or six times throughout the course of the show is almost guaranteed to piss off the people that hired you and ensure that you don't get asked back. Do not make your entire presentation about selling product; you are already being paid, sales after the show are a bonus on top of the paycheck.

Mailing List

We touched on mailing lists and their importance earlier. Have a signup sheet on your sales table and encourage people to join your list. This is one of the best ways to garner dedicated fans, and the next time you perform in the area, it is likely those fans will bring new people to the show. Having toured to libraries and returned several years in a row, it is entirely possible to have fifty people at a show the first year, and two hundred people show up the next.

Getting Re-Hired

Several of the librarians had very good advice on what makes a performer more likely to get re-hired.

Tom Cooper, Director of the Webster Groves Public Library:

Performers that show an understanding that a library, as a venue, is different from a theater or other places they may perform, and that the reason they are there is to enhance the library's mission and outreach to its community are more likely to be brought back for future performances.

Sue Ridnour, Director of Library Services at the Flower Mound Public Library offered this:

There are a few things that would make me say 'I will never bring that group back again. Primary among them are banter that is inappropriate for the age of the audience, or disrespectful or insulting to the audience in any way, [particularly] if the audience includes children or younger teens, who don't always understand sarcasm. The second is showing up late, or being unprepared in a way that causes the show to start late. Libraries, like schools, are often operating on a fairly rigid time schedule.

Heather Backman, the Adult Services Librarian at the Hopkinton Public Library had this to say:

Strong attendance and patron comments are a big motivator for me in booking or re-booking presenters.

Almost all of the librarians agreed that if a performer is engaging, organized, polite, reasonably adept at their program and on-time they are much more likely to be asked back to perform again.

NOTES

DOCUMENTS & TOOLS TO MAKE LIFE EASIER

You're touring, you're on the road, and the library asks you for a document while you're stuck in a hotel room somewhere with no access to a printer. Wouldn't it be easier to have the documents already at your fingertips, an email or a click away?

Tools:

1. Dropbox, Google Docs, iCloud, or the equivalent. Having access to documents online at the click of a button while you're out on tour is priceless and will save you time and frustration. I'm going to refer to Dropbox from here out, because that's what I use. Most of these services are fairly equivalent though.

2. Adobe Acrobat Professional – this will allow you to fill out .pdf documents right from your computer without having to print them first. You can even sign documents electronically this way.

3. An iPad or the equivalent. A touchscreen tablet will also allow you to sign documents without having to print them out first. On the iPad a

program called Notability is my favorite for this purpose.

4. A smartphone. Yes, they're more expensive, yes there are sometimes signal issues, but overall they will help a lot more than they hinder. Something to consider as an add-on to a smart phone is a mobile hot-spot. This will allow your laptop to have wireless internet connection if you have any cell signal. If you get a mobile hotspot make sure there is a hefty data plan attached.

5. A GPS separate from your phone. If you are driving regularly for your tours a GPS is great. They can usually calculate (with some degree of accuracy) how long it will take you to get somewhere, give you directions, and they work in areas where your cell phone does not have signal.

Apps for Smartphone Users

1. **Gas Buddy** – This is a free app that allows you to locate gas stations and see what gas prices are in the nearby area. Gas prices are updated by the users when they stop at a gas station.

2. **Receipt Catcher** – This 99 cent app allows you to take photos of your receipts, log the information and email yourself a report at the end of each month. Downside – if you download a new version it wipes out all of your existing data, so make sure to email the reports to yourself before doing any updates.

3. **Cleartune Chromatic Tuner** – A $3.99 app for the musicians. Never be without a tuner!

4. **Decibel 10th or Decibels** – Both are apps designed to measure the noise level. This is great for musicians who may or may not need to worry about noise ordinances.

5. **Square or PayPal** – Both of these apps allow you to take credit card payments and come with a card reader. (The company will mail it to you after you sign up for service.)

Documents to have on hand:

1. W9 – Request for Taxpayer Identification Number – after a contract, this is the most common document needed to get a check cut. Fill it out in advance, scan a copy and save it in your Dropbox.

2. Invoice – create a template for an invoice (Microsoft Word has several templates available if you don't want to create one from scratch.) Make sure it has your mailing address, phone number, website, and space for the details about the show. Save the template in your Dropbox and access it whenever a library asks for an invoice.

Contract – have a blank copy of your contract saved in your Dropbox in case you book shows while you're on the road. Then you can fill it out immediately and get it sent to the venue before you forget.

NOTES

FRIENDS OF THE LIBRARY

You may hear the term Friends of the Library – typically this is a group of community members that work with the library, supporting the library with extra funds, volunteers, ideas and fundraisers. In many cases, the Friends of the Library is also the group that pays for programing. If the person scheduling programing is a volunteer, or a member of the Friends group, that typically means that they work in off hours, evenings, or weekends as they have time. They are outside the structure of the library, and may be difficult to get in touch with.

The Friends of the Library is part of a national group called United for Libraries. Most states will have a chapter. Addresses for the state chapter organizations can be found on the American Library Association website at: http://www.ala.org/united/friends/statefriends

Some of the links in the state chapter directory will provide the names/addresses/phone numbers for local chapters. As you are working on booking gigs, if the library says 'our Friends group handles that' you now have a way to contact the Friends group.

If you are booked at the library through the Friends of the Library, remember to thank them and encourage people in the audience to sign up. The library always needs more friends.

Authors take note: there is a special program through United for Libraries called Authors for Libraries. (http://authorsforlibraries.org/)At the time of this writing it cost $39 to join and proposes to help with scheduling library talks and signings. I have not yet used this service, but it looks promising. They have a listserv specifically for authors and libraries, per their website, "[it] invites authors, librarians, and other interested individuals to exchange ideas, information, opportunities for author programs, announcements of new books, and more."

NOTES

PERFORMER SHOWCASES

As a professional performer you are likely familiar with showcasing. Showcasing is where a variety of performers show up and perform for eight to fifteen minutes in front of an audience of prospective venue representatives with the intention of securing future gigs. Showcases can be a goldmine of opportunity, particularly if you tour frequently in the region. However, if you only tour in an area once a year, or your availability in that area is extremely limited it may not be worth your time and energy.

There are library showcases throughout the United States, but they are frequently hard to find. Performers that know about them apply, so the library has very little need to advertise the dates/times or locations to find new performers.

The vast majority of performer showcases for libraries are aimed at children's programs. There is usually an application process, and there is sometimes a fee associated. Keep that in mind if you decide to showcase – if the event is only aimed at children's programs, and you don't do children's programs, don't waste your time and money, and don't take the slot away from someone else who may benefit from it. How do you know who the showcase is aimed at? If it is not immediately evident from the application, ask.

If you decide to showcase, in addition to the performance itself:

❖ Be prepared to provide flyers for each of the showcase attendees – frequently the organizers will ask for these in advance and prepare packets.

❖ Know your touring schedule and have a copy of it on-hand with you. A paper copy is fine as long as it's current. Some of the venues will make an immediate decision and may want to schedule a program (or multiple programs) with you that day.

❖ Have plenty of business cards on hand. If you have other promotional materials (free download cards, sample CDs or videos etc.) bring them and hand them out. Everyone likes free stuff.

A showcase performance for libraries should include the following (edit the length of each depending on the time allotted):

1. A brief introduction – who you are, what you do, why you're great for the age group you perform for. No more than two minutes.

2. A representative and memorable demonstration of your program. You will not have time to do an entire program, so choose the highlights. (Five to ten minutes)

3. Closing – let them know if you are giving discounts to people who schedule at the showcase, point out your flyer to them, tell them how to contact you, and if you have a booth at the showcase, where your booth is located.

Do not go over your allotted time.

As you go through the showcase day, hand out and collect as many business cards, email addresses, and names as you can. Before and after your time slot, it's all about networking.

Some of the showcases will provide a list with venue and program coordinator contact information either in email form, or handed out as a list at the event. If you acquire such a document, treat it as pure gold. Follow up with everyone on that list.

Below is a list of libraries and areas that host regular showcases. It is by no means a complete list, but will give you a place to start.

- ❖ **Arizona** - Artists and Performer's Expo – they also have an online directory associated with the event.
- ❖ **California**:
  - o Association of Children's Librarians of Northern California
  - o Southern California Library Cooperative at the Yorba Linda Public Library – they provide a directory of performers to librarians after the event.
- ❖ **Colorado** - Colorado Performing Arts Jamboree
- ❖ **Florida** –at the Florida Library Association Conference. They also have a performer directory associated with the showcase. There is an entry fee.
- ❖ **Iowa** Library Services – Contact the State Library
- ❖ **Missouri** Library Association – at the Missouri Library Association conference
- ❖ **New York** - Westchester Library System
- ❖ **Oregon** – Contact the Oregon Library Association's Children's Services Section
- ❖ **Pennsylvania** –at the Pennsylvania Library Conference. They also have a performer directory associated with the showcase
- ❖ **South Carolina** – Contact the South Carolina State Library

❖ **Texas**
- o Central Texas Library System – There is a fee for this showcase.
- o Fort Worth Performer Showcase
- o North Texas Library System
  - North Texas Conference for Library Program Planners & Presenters (Fee assoc.)

NOTES

NOTES

PERFORMER DATABASES & DIRECTORIES

Library performer databases are essentially a place to list yourself or your group, contact information, prices, website, and program descriptions. It is an online or physical catalog for librarians to browse and search for performers. There are a number of these around, but no overarching national one specifically for libraries. Once you set yourself up in these databases you can (unless your contact information changes) leave them alone. The more exposure, the more likely you are to get gigs. Keep a list somewhere of which databases you have information in – it makes it easier when you have to update the information. As a reminder, advertising is great; advertising and setting yourself up in a directory for a place you will never visit is bad form.

Some of the library performer databases currently in operation are:

❖ **Arizona** –
http://www.lib.az.us/carnegie/showcase/showcase_entry.aspx

- ❖ **Chicago** – This is a for-profit group. https://www.premier-showcase.com/index.php
- ❖ **Florida** – Library association performers directory. Contact the library association. There is a fee.
- ❖ **Georgia** – A librarian has to add you to this Children's Performer database. http://www.georgialibraries.org/lib/child/childdirect ory.php
- ❖ **Massachusetts** – http://mblc.state.ma.us/advisory/performer/
- ❖ **New York** State Performers & Programs Database http://www.performersandprograms.com/
- ❖ **Texas** - NTLP – Not Typical Library Partners http://nottypical.org/presentersdirectory

There are undoubtedly more of these directories out there, and they change over time as websites and employees come and go. They are an easy way of getting your name out there and increasing your web presence.

LISTSERVS
Per Wikipedia:
The term Listserv has been used to refer to a few early electronic mailing list software applications, allowing a sender to send one email to the list, and then transparently sending it on to the addresses of the subscribers to the list.

The Listserv is alive and well in library land, and there are quite a few of them that see regular and heavy use. They are usually operated state by state, though there is one national one that I am aware of. Most of the listservs are not specifically dealing with programing, but rather are a place for librarians to ask questions of other librarians. Some of them will allow non-librarians to join. Most of the librarian listservs will allow you to ask questions, and most of them frown strongly on people using them to advertise.

If you decide to look into the listservs, I highly

recommend setting up a separate email account specifically for that purpose as, on average, the busy listservs generate several hundred emails a week.

NOTES

A FEW FINAL SUGGESTIONS

The life of a full time, touring, living wage performer is something that most people take up for love of the art. What many of the successful living wage performers do is treat it as a small business. As a small business owner, where *you* are the primary product, it is important to remember to take care of yourself financially, spiritually (if that is your style) and health-wise.

Financially

Plan your tours so that they are financially profitable as often as possible. Driving from Texas to Maine for one $300 performance is not profitable. (Unless performing this show will then garner you several higher paid shows, or allow you to meet people who schedule such shows.)

Sit down before you leave on a tour and figure out approximately how much money you will spend on:

❖ Gas and transportation
  o Figure out how many miles your touring vehicle gets on a tank of gas. (Lets say 300 miles)
  o Map out how many miles the entire tour will be. (For this tour – 1,200 miles.)
  o Divide the number of touring miles by the

number of miles per tank of gas. (1,200 ÷ 300 = 4 tanks of gas.)You now know how many tanks of gas it will take (approximately) for the tour.

- o Multiply how many tanks of gas (4) by how much a normal tank of gas costs ($50 for this example) (4x50 = $200 in gas money.)
- o I'd recommend adding an extra tank of gas to this just for planning purposes.

❖ Food

- o Figure out a food budget and try to stick to it. Do you really need to eat out at a restaurant every day, or can you bring a cooler or ice chest with you to save on food costs? What many of the performers I worked with did or recommended was to have an ice chest for things that needed to stay cool – healthy snacks, veggies, fruits, yogurt or other perishables, and then have a food bag for dry goods – a loaf of bread, granola bars, power bars, other snacks that don't need refrigeration. That way you buy these items at a store before leaving on tour, rather than at the considerably more expensive gas station.

  One group went so far as to bring a handheld blender to make nutritious fruit shakes for breakfast every morning. They then also used the frozen fruit to help cool their cooler during the day.

  Think smarter about food and food consumption.

❖ Lodging

- o This is one of the most expensive parts of touring. See if the venues will pay for your hotel room. If you must pay for your own, booking your hotels more than 6-8 weeks in advance can save you money.

❖ Replacement equipment (Strings for guitars etc.)

Other Financial Tips

❖ Consider finding a low interest credit card that accrues points that can be used for cash back, free hotel nights, or free flights. Use this only for touring expenses and then PAY IT OFF EVERY MONTH! This will also help track what your touring expenses are, and makes tax time a little bit easier.

❖ Get on the rewards program for whichever hotel chain you prefer and when you can't find free lodging, stay at that type of hotel to accrue upgrades and free nights.

❖ Take advantage of the Starbucks Rewards program, and sandwich shop or restaurant 'frequent flyer' cards. They are a bit of a pain to keep track of (except Starbucks, there's an app for that!) but they do mean free food.

Spiritually

Take time for yourself, take time to practice your faith, take time to study and learn new things – whatever it is that rejuvenates you, don't let being on the road take that away from you. Groups that tour together successfully learn that they cannot all be in the same place all the time. It is important for each individual to take time for themselves away from the group. This helps to diffuse tension, reduce stress and prevent some arguments.

Particularly on long or busy tours it is important to have a rest day at least once a week. If nothing else, you will need to do laundry. Plan those times into the tour, and give yourself a day to relax. Don't use that day to catch up on booking, use that day to read a book, or visit the local sights or just get out of the hotel room and the car and walk around.

Remember, you have chosen this type of life, which is

different than the standard 8:00 – 5:00 office job and offers many freedoms not available to others. Take advantage of the benefits this affords you. Going to Washington, DC? Take a day to see the sights. Driving through Arizona? Take a day to stop and see the Grand Canyon.

In addition to taking time for yourself, take time for the group as a whole to do fun things together. Visit an arcade, have ping pong tournaments in the hotel room, socialize and talk about something other than work.

Taking care of yourself and your group will help reduce tension and prevent arguments from developing as quickly.

Health Wise

If you haven't got your health what have you got? Touring is stressful and hard on the immune system, and head colds make it really difficult to perform at gigs. While there is no way to entirely avoid getting sick while on tour there are a few things you can do to help yourself:

❖ <u>Get enough sleep</u>. I cannot emphasize this enough.

❖ Bring your own pillow from home and use it instead of the hotel pillows. Having something from home may help promote better sleep, it is a familiar object, and with hotels it's hit or miss as to the quality of the pillows anyway. As a bonus, if you're couch surfing you don't have to depend on your host for a pillow. This is particularly helpful when your host has pets that   you   are   allergic   to.

❖ If there is something that helps you sleep better, bring it along! Sleep is a hot commodity when on the road.

❖ Eat at least two healthy meals a day. (Don't always pick McDonalds, sometimes go for the salad bar at Subway, or occasionally splurge for a real meal!)

❖ <u>Bathe every day.</u>

❖ Wash your hands frequently. (Doubly so if you perform around children!)

❖ Use hand sanitizer.

❖ Avoid touching your face, eyes, nose and mouth as much as possible.

❖ Drink plenty of water! (Not coffee, or tea, or soda, or energy drinks; water! It's okay to drink the other things too, but they are not as good at keeping you hydrated. Consider drinking one glass of water for every cup of something else you drink.)

❖ Take multi-vitamins.

❖ Bring an ice-chest for cold food and a bag for other food. Include healthy snacks as well as comfort food. Avoid shopping for said food at gas stations or convenience stores.

❖ It is not necessary to partake of every dessert bar that every venue sets out for you.

❖ Use the hotel workout rooms, or develop your own workout routine. When touring you spend a *lot* of time sitting in cars or driving. It is important to make the body move, stretch and work to maintain flexibility and health. (This can also help with back pain that may develop due to sitting in a car seat for long periods at a time.)

❖ If you're not one for workouts, try walking places instead of driving when you take the day off.

❖ Spend time away from other members of the group. (This will help your sanity, and cut down on arguments!)

❖ Bring a small medicine kit with you on the road. Basics should include:
  o Pepto-Bismol and/or Tums
  o Ibuprofen, Aspirin or Tylenol
  o Cold medication
  o Cough drops or sore throat drops
  o Band aids and antiseptic
  o Allergy medication
  o A small sewing kit (surprisingly useful!)
  o Eye drops
  o Extra contact solution & lenses, or extra eye glasses
  o A list of prescription medications everyone takes.

The business of being a professional touring performer is frequently as challenging as it is rewarding. The information found in the first half of this book primarily discusses working with libraries, but is applicable to schools, community centers, museums and other small venues as well. The information on touring and retaining your sanity is applicable to almost anyone that travels on the road with companions for long periods of time. As you plan your tours, whether you are an old hat at the touring business or just starting out, I encourage you to take up practices that will keep you healthy and creating your art for years to come.

I hope that you have found this book helpful and informative and that it improves your life on the road. I am no longer running an agency, but if you would like to be in touch, or find out what other projects I am working on, please contact me through my website at: www.jessicabrawner.com

NOTES

NOTES

RESOURCES

Websites
Computer Related
- o   LibreOffice http://www.libreoffice.org/
- o   Dropbox https://www.dropbox.com/

Sample Contracts
- o   Sample contracts in this book can be found at www.jessicabrawner.com

Library Related
- o   American Library Association http://www.ala.org/
- o   Institute of Museum and Library Services http://www.imls.gov/
- o   Public Libraries.com http://www.publiclibraries.com
- o   United for Libraries http://www.ala.org/united/friends/statefriends

Performer Databases
- o   Arizona – http://www.lib.az.us/carnegie/showcase/showca se_entry.aspx
- o   Chicago –https://www.premier-showcase.com/index.php
- o   Georgia – http://www.georgialibraries.org/lib/child/childdi rectory.php
- o   Massachusetts – http://mblc.state.ma.us/advisory/performer/
- o   New York State Performers & Programs Database http://www.performersandprograms.com/
- o   Texas - NTLP – http://nottypical.org/presentersdirectory

Mailing List Related

o   Constant Contact
http://www.constantcontact.com/
o   Direct Mail http://directmailmac.com/
o   Mail Chimp http://mailchimp.com/
o   Your Mailing List Provider
https://www.ymlp.com/
o   Benchmark Mail
http://www.benchmarkemail.com/
o   Mad Mimi https://www.madmimi.com

Music & Touring Related

o   Artist Data http://www.artistdata.com/us/
o   Sonic Bids http://www.sonicbids.com/

SAMPLES

Phone Script – Initial Conversation

You: "Hi! My name is _____. I'm with [**insert your group name here**]. We're a [**group type i.e. folk music duo, juggling act, science education group**]. We'll be travelling through your area [**insert dates here**] and wanted to see if you would be interested in having us perform at your library."

Librarian: "I've never heard of you. Do you have a website?"

You: "Yes! Our web address is [**insert your website**] and I'd be happy to email you some information as well. Can I get your email address?"

Librarian: "Sure, my email address is xxxxx@library.tx.us"

You: "Great! I'll email that information over right away. When would be a good time to follow up with you?"

Librarian: "Check back with me in a couple of weeks, that's when I'll be working on booking our [fall, spring, summer, winter] programing."

You: "Would you prefer an email follow up, or a phone call?"

Program Description

Instrument Education Concert for children of all ages – material to be selected based on maturity/age level:

About the group

As a duo, Bettman & Halpin are fast earning a reputation for hypnotizing performances filled with irresistible lyrics, transcendent harmonies and roof-raising instrumentals. Their music creates a fully acoustic, delightfully eclectic sound far greater than the sum of its parts: taking the listener from up-tempo down home fiddlin', to soulful sorrowful ballads, to super hooky folk/pop with catchy melodies and lyrics that will stick with you long after the concert is over.

About the program

For this program Bettman & Halpin perform a short concert (30 – 45 min) for children's groups, with a question and answer session afterwards. This is approximately a one-hour program. During the concert they take some time in between songs to talk about their instruments, how they started writing music, the history of folk and bluegrass music etc. and answer questions from the participants as they arise.

This program meets and supports the following Academic Standards in the state of Colorado for grades 9-12:

Academic Standards

o Theory of Music: Classification by genre, style, historical period, or culture.

o Aesthetic Valuation of Music:

- Practice of appropriate behavior during cultural activities.
- Knowledge of available musical opportunities for continued musical growth and professional development.

Contact information

To find out about more of our programs, or schedule a performance please visit our website at www.[insertwebaddresshere].com or give us a call at (123) 555-4567.

Follow Up Email

Dear Tammy,

Thank you for taking the time to speak with me this afternoon. My group, Sampson and Delilah Juggling, will be touring through your area June 5-7, 2016. You can find out more about the group on our website at www.[insertwebaddresshere].com

Attached please find a listing of the different programs we offer, along with descriptions and recommended age groups for each.

If you have any questions, or would like to schedule a performance, please contact me at performer@emailaddresshere.com or by phone at (123) 555-4567.

I look forward to hearing from you soon.

[Your Name]
Phone: (123) 555-4567
Email: performer@emailaddresshere.com
Website: www.[insertwebaddresshere].com

SAMPLE CONTRACT 1
LETTER OF AGREEMENT

This agreement is between [PERFORMER] and [VENUE]. On [DATE] [PERFORMER] will perform at [VENUE] from [BLOCK OF TIME] Admission will be $_____. [PERFORMER]will be paid $_____ for presentation. **The presentation fee will be paid upon completion of the performance unless prior arrangements have been made.**
Payment should be made out to [PERFORMER].

The [VENUE] will advertise by putting out flyers, and through email and/or online calendars as is appropriate.

[PERFORMER] will advertise by listing performance on calendars, websites, Press Releases etc.

[PERFORMER] will be allowed to sell CDs, T-shirts and other items related to the program at the [VENUE].

ARTIST REQUIREMENTS

List anything you __need__ the venue to provide. Items might include bottled water, digital projector, electrical outlets, music stands, podium, basically anything that you can't provide yourself. Remember, libraries can't usually provide much, but it ALWAYS helps to ask in advance. Asking when you show up and not in advance is a recipe for disaster.

[PERFORMER] will ensure performance barring injury, illness, death and acts of God. [VENUE] will provide performance space barring all of the above. [VENUE] will be liable for payment if [PERFORMER] is not informed of schedule changes within 5 business days of the performance. [PERFORMER] will notify [VENUE] of any and all changes as soon as information is available. [PERFORMER] will do their best to notify [VENUE] of any cancellation with at least 48 hours notice if possible. If [PERFORMER] is unable to perform for reasons cause by or relating to themselves [VENUE] will NOT be required to pay for the performance.

[PERFORMER] will arrive 1 to 1.5 hours before the performance to prepare the performance space.

By signing below both parties are in agreement. Any and all disputes will be handled by professional mediation if necessary.

_____   _____
[PERFORMER] [DATE]   [VENUE] [DATE]

94

SAMPLE CONTRACT 2

PERFORMER NAME
ADDRESS
PHONE

Performer:_____

Name of Act: (if applicable)_____

Venue address:_____

City:_____ State_____ Zip_____

Phone:_____

Contact Person:_____

Email Address:_____

****

Compensation:

[VENUE] will pay [PERFORMER] $_____ for
the following performance :

List a brief description of the performance including:

Performance Title:_____

Length of Performance: _____

Number of performances per day:_____

Requested performance dates: _____

Performance fee will be paid at the time of the
performance.

_____

[VENUE REPRESENTATIVE]   [DATE]

_____

[PERFORMER REPRESENTATIVE]   [DATE]

Electronic Filing System
Folder 1: Group Name
> **Folder 2: Booking Information**
>> **Folder 3: 2014** (Information for gigs happening in that year. Each year, create a new folder.)
>>> **Folder 4: 2014 10 3 (Cleveland OH)** (Year, month, day, city, state)

Other useful folders
> **Folder 2: Press Materials**
>> **Folder 3: Press Photos** – Professional photos of you and/or your group suitable for publication in print and online. Press photos should be at a minimum 2MB in size.
>>
>> **Folder 3: Press Releases** –Standard press release that you can edit to include the venue's name and the performance time/location.
>>
>> **Folder 3: Letters of Recommendation**
>
> **Folder 2: Tax and Accounting Forms** – store your W9, an invoice template, a blank contract, and any other forms that you use on a regular basis, or that you will need to send to the venue in this folder.
>
> **Folder 2: Contact and Mailing Lists** – keep a spreadsheet backup of your contacts and/or your mailing lists.

ABOUT THE AUTHOR

Jessica Brawner sprouted in the wilds of South Texas and plotted ways to spend her life traveling the world. She has been remarkably successful at that endeavor, and is now based in the Front Range region of Colorado. In addition to her writing activities, Ms. Brawner has developed and taught self-defense classes, owned an entertainment agency and worked as an agent, and worked as an event planner, a computer teacher, and a personal assistant. Her newest venture, in addition to her writing, is Story of the Month Club – Excellent Stories To Your Inbox (www.storyofthemonthclub.com).

You can find out more about Ms. Brawner and her activities at www.jessicabrawner.com

Made in the USA
San Bernardino, CA
19 September 2016